Starting Over

Starting Over

Jacqueline Allen

Superior Publishing LLC.

CONTENTS

	DEDICATION	vii
1	BECAUSE HE LIVES	1
2	STARTING OVER ANEW	6
3	A FRESH BEGINNING	10
4	A NEW MIND	13
5	PRAISE HIM	17
6	WE ARE VICTORIOUS	20
7	FOOD FOR THOUGHT	23
8	STAND FIRM!	27
9	GOD NAMED US	30
10	GOD OPENED MY EYES	33
11	GOD WILL CARRY US THROUGH	36

| v |

CONTENTS

12 FALL BACK AND SPRING FORWARD 39

photo insert 42

references 43

*This book is dedicated to my biggest supporters!
Some are gone but will never be forgotten.
Their words will live with me forever.
James and Annie Pierce
John Rogers
Maria Taylor
Martha N. Bean*

Copyright © 2022 by Jacqueline Allen
All rights reserved. No part of this book may be reproduced in any manner whatsoever without written permission except in the case of brief quotations embodied in critical articles and reviews.

SUPERIOR PUBLISHING LLC 2022
Cedar Bluff, MS
(662) 295-9893

1

BECAUSE HE LIVES

Jesus died and rose again on the third day. And because of that we can live also. God wrote us a love letter, the Bible, and all we have to do is live by it.

Don't put yourself down, walk in the glory of God. His mercy is renewed every day. When He created you, He didn't create junk! He created you in His image. I used to sit and listen to people talk about me saying that I wouldn't amount to anything and on the inside, my heart would just break because it was the people that I loved so much putting me down. But now I can look at them and smile because Jesus lives. I am everything He said I could be.

God has a plan for us

Even though I knew God had a plan for me, their words would still hurt me. So, what I had to do, was pull out my love letter and find out who I truly was and then I found out that I could do all things through Jesus. Philippians 4:13 I can do all things through Christ who strengthens me.

This song always lifted me up, "Because He lives" Because He lives you can face tomorrow because all fear is gone. He holds your future. Isn't it a wonderful feeling to know that God, not man but God holds your future?

The song says because He lives all fear is gone. So, what's holding you back or what is it that you are afraid of? What is keeping you from jumping on that Glory train with Jesus? I promise, you will not regret it.

This world we live in is so dark because of the evil that we face. We need Jesus every second, minute and hour of the day. I have walked these old rugged roads with my head hung low and I have stood at the crossroad not knowing which way to go. I was at a very dark time in my life and I could not even see no light in sight. Once I accepted Jesus as my personal Lord and Savior my whole life changed forever. Laying down my life and picking up my cross was the best decision I ever made in my life and now I can truly say, "Because He lives, I truly can face my tomorrow and anything else that comes against me.

Jesus is the Giver of true joy, "The World has its joy, but the joy of Jesus gives will never change. In your good times rejoice in Jesus, also rejoice in your bad times. Because He lives you can face tomorrow and anything else that comes against you. Let your light so shine so bright that it will draw others to Jesus. We have hope to keep us alive and going strong. True hope that only Jesus can give.

HOPE

What is hope? It is to cherish a desire with anticipation- to want something to be true. Things have a way of coming upon us and against us that we have no control over.

BUT we can HOPE! God never said that weapon wouldn't form, but we can find hope and comfort in knowing that it will not harm us. Isaiah 54:17

John 14:27, Jesus tells us that our troubles are passing in nature for a season and a reason. Our hope comes from Him telling us to let not our hearts be troubled. We have to hold on to the peace that God gives us. God is saying to us in Isaiah 26:3, we will keep perfect peace who trust in Him. There is hope in knowing who God is and how much He loves you. There is hope in knowing that we can face anything because of the power of the cross. There is hope in praising God because when the praises go up the blessings come down. There were times that I didn't even know where I was going to lay my head or where my next meal was coming from, there were times I did not knowing how I was going to pay my bills, but because of my hope and my faith in God, He always came through for me. He never came through for me when I wanted Him to but, He was always on time. Because Jesus lives, we have renewed hope every day.

Stop putting yourself down, start walking in the glory of God. When He created you, He created you in His image. He has a plan and a purpose for you. Don't be defined by your pain, there's going to be some mountains to climb, some oceans to cross and some dark valley to walk through but there is hope in knowing that you are not alone. When God see you the only thing, he sees His Son on the cross, perfect, holy and covered in righteousness. God calls us beloved, chosen friend, son, daughter, lovely and wanted. See yourself how God sees you.

HOPE

Psalm 42:11 hope in God and praise Him who is the of your countenance and your God.

1Peter 1:21 God raised Jesus from the dead so we can put our faith and hope in Him

1Peter 1:13 Wherefore gird up the loins of your mind, be sober and hope to the end for the grace that is to be brought unto you at the revelation of Jesus Christ.

1 John 3: 3 Every man that has this hope in Him purifieth himself even as he is pure.

Proverbs 14:32 The Wicked is driven away in is wickedness, but the righteous hath hope in his death.

Colossians 1:27 Which is Christ in you, the hope of glory.

Psalm 31:24 Be ye of good courage and He shall strengthen your heart all ye that hope in the Lord.

Psalm 71:5 for thou art my hope, O Lord God; thou art my trust from my youth.

Don't ever give up on hoping that things are going to get better because they will. You've got to believe in what you are hoping for. Jesus is our true HOPE and He is with you always. Hebrews 13:5 God said, He will never leave you, He will never forsake you. 6. God is your Helper you do not have to be afraid. Knowing that God is always with you is enough to keep hope alive in your life.

TO GOD BE ALL THE GLORY!
JACQUELINE ALLEN

2

STARTING OVER ANEW

BEING SET FREE

After writing my first book, it brought freedom to me. The things that once held me bound, no longer had control over me. And for the first time in my life, I felt alive and free. I was set free from the pains that held me bound. I feel peace and I am finally able to breathe again.

Well as you know the devil don't like it when we win over him, when he loses one of his soldiers, he gets mad because he doesn't want to see us successful. He will use anything and anyone anywhere and anytime to try and get us off track. We have to stay focused on God. He knows the plans that He has for us.

Pray, Praise and Push my friend!
Praise and Push Yourself Forward
NO
  LOOKING
    BACK!

STARTING OVER

It's not going to be easy starting over not on your own. But it will be worth leaving the past behind and walking with God. There is so much that gets thrown at us in this life and we sometimes fail in our faith because of all the stress. God's word is our refuge. There is nothing God cannot protect us from.

Once God has delivered us from something that has been holding us back and He gives us the strength to deal with the moments and minutes of life, it is time to walk forward in your new life. We have to start over again, Philippians 1:21, for me to live is Christ and to die is gain. Philippians 3:7 what things were gain to me I count a loss for Christ. In order to move on to the future, Philippians 3:13-14 tells us to forget what is behind and reach forward to those things which are before. 14. Press toward the mark for the prize of the high calling of God in Christ Jesus. 21. Tells us that God can change our body that it may be fashioned like unto his glorious body.

We have to start over again in the freedom that God is blessing us with. John 8:36 tells us if the Son sets you free then you are free indeed and we have to start to rejoice in our freedom of starting over. Philippians 4:4 Rejoice in the Lord always. I will say it again Rejoice. 5. Let your gentleness be evident to all that God is near.

Once God gives you that special peace, Philippians 4:6 the peace that surpasses all understanding and it will guard your heart and minds in Christ Jesus. That special peace that no man can give and no man should be allowed to take it away. Now, you have a choice as to whether you give it up or not. Sometimes I look back on all the pain that I faced in life and I know the anger and bitterness that it brought on me, I have no desire to go back and live in that time. I have made up my mind that since God loved me enough to save me, it might not mean anything to anyone else, but for me, every time God has allowed me to open my eyes day after day, with renewed grace and mercy it means everything to me. I have decided that my mind is made up that I am not going to allow anyone or anything to interfere with the peace that God has given me to start my life over again. He will give it to you also a peace that will guard your heart and your mind in Jesus Christ.

After being set free, you learn to see differently, talk differently and act differently. Starting over and moving forward don't mean to travel back on the same roads. It is time for something new! We need new friends, God given friends that will encourage you, walk with you and not turn you away when things are not going the way they want them. But friends that know God and can and will pray for you. I have found out that everything that happens in life happens for a reason. It can strengthen us or break us; it depends on how we handle it.

Since starting over, I have come to realize that God is in control and I have been set free from my old ways of thinking. God knows the plans He has for us. And there is no what if, in His plan. We have to believe that it will work. The things that once held me down doesn't have power over me anymore. A new mind, a new walk, and a new destination.

Thank You Lord for Your renewed Grace and Mercy. Starting over we have to surround ourselves with positive people who build us up not tear us down. People that speak life into us. We can find joy as we celebrate our freedom. When you embrace the freedom and love of God there is nothing that can stop you.

As you start over remember:
Psalm 91: 14-15 God deliver and answers
Psalm 118:5 God answers
Psalm 119:45 We can walk in freedom

Isaiah 61:1 God has anointed us
John 8:32 The truth will free you
John 10:10 Jesus came to give life
Romans 8:16 the Spirit bears witness for us.

I said it once, I will say it again, if you don't leave the past behind you will never make room for your present and future.

3

A FRESH BEGINNING

This is the day that the Lord has made, let us rejoice and be glad in it, Philippians 4:19.

A new day with a fresh outlook and a restored heart. Now that we know that God loves and cares for us and that He is the light on our dark days and our guide when we are lost, it should not matter how other feel about us. God knows the plan that He has for us, plans to prosper and not harm you, hope and a future, Jeremiah 29:11.

Knowing all of this, should be enough to make us choose God and not worry about things and people that are coming against us. Like I said before, it is time to encourage yourself in God's word and think about what He thinks about us and to listen to the things that He's saying to us. If we are always sitting around complaining and putting ourselves down then others are going to do it as well.

With this fresh start, you got to know who you are. You need to know that you are blessed and highly favored. You need to know that you are the son/daughter of the King. You need to know that you are the head and not the tail. You need to know that you are God's Chosen and that you need to encourage someone else and let

STARTING OVER

them know who they are to God. We are the only bible that some people will ever read. So, let's be that light shining on the hill for everyone to see.

Surround yourself with positive people, those that will cheer you on because everyone is not going support you or be glad about your progress. I thank God for my sister Lori Dreux and for the wisdom and knowledge that God has blessed her with. Even though we are separated by miles and miles, God always keeps us close. She's always just a call away. Sometimes she just listens and other times she encourages me to always just take another step. We encourage each other to push forward. She doesn't mind telling me when I am wrong and we all need that special someone in our lives. There are people that God will put in our lives at just the right time.

Thank you, Sister Amy, for the extra push that as kept me smiling, and moving forward. I thank my Pastor, Pastor Boddie for always encouraging me. We have to keep a 3wsZheart and mind so when God sends that special person, we won't push them away.

Going through the pain helped me to welcome my fresh start. I shut people out because of my negative mind and I didn't want to face the hurt of what they might say. Starting over helped me to see that everyone was not against me.

Thank You Lord for working on me and helping me to see that it is truly some good peoples that are only trying to build up and not tear down. Trying to be a help and not harm. There comes a time that we have to thank and praise God for the ones that we have in our lives. There are some rare kinds of people who care enough to allow and even encourage you to be who you are but encourage you to be better. They don't look down on you, they pray for you and with you. They cry with you and for you. Ask God to send that rare person into your life to help guide you to the right road that you are seeking.

As it says, 2 Peter 1:5-8, there are several qualities that every Christian must possess to keep from being ineffective and unproductive in the knowledge of our Lord Jesus Christ and we can learn from those people. A true friend will tell you that despite what you see around you, you can still be productive and have an effective Christian life. They will give you their knowledge of what they know to be true, right and pure to help you to see things in a different way.

Being around positive people will make you want to succeed because their knowledge, perseverance, and faith will make you want to get on the right track. They will help you aim for Godliness, keeping your mind focused on God's Word to help make you a better person.

I fall sometimes but I know I can get back u and so can you. The race is not over I am urging you to keep on keeping on.

4

A NEW MIND

Once we realize that our thoughts are not the way God wants us to think, we need to tell ourselves that it is time to start making our thoughts line up with God's. God's word help us to know His thoughts.

Romans 12:2, tells us not to conform to the pattern of this world but be ye transformed by the renewing of our minds. It is time for us to really think about what we are thinking about. You can't think negative and get a positive result. Philippians 2:5, In order for us to have a new positive outlook on our lives and get a positive result we have to start thinking and acting different.

Don't hold on to the thoughts of yesterday. Find out what God wants you to think about today! Our thoughts begin with our way of thinking. Think negative, get negative, think positive and get positive. 1 Corinthians 2:16 tell us that we have the mind of Christ. So, we must try to see things as Jesus see them. When we look at others, we only see them the way we want to see them but, we have to learn to look at them with our Christ like mind.

God doesn't want us to focus on the thoughts of the past or what might happen tomorrow. He wants you to see today and focus on Him and learn how to praise Him today. If you are focused on yesterday or looking for things on tomorrow you are missing out on today.

Sometimes we get so busy worrying about how others see us that we soon forget about God really sees us. When someone is talking about you and it's not lining up with God's word, then it doesn't matter what they are saying because it does not concern you.

As a young girl growing up, I would hear all kinds of negative talk about me and the words would really hurt but as I grew in my relationship with God, I found myself doing things that would prove them wrong about me and prove God right.

I just want to take this moment and say, "Thank You Lord for being there to protect and watch over me, because some of the things I did to prove them wrong could have caused me my life, but Lord, you never left me alone, you lit my path."

We have to walk away from people who never have a positive word because what they are saying is neither lifting us up or helping us in anyway. I was weak in my own strength, but I found strength in what God said about my strength.

Isaiah 40:31, those who wait on the Lord will renew their strength. They will soar on wings like eagles; they will run and not grow weary. And then, Philippians 4:13 says I can do all things through Christ who strengthens me.

I had to fix my mind and heart on things above reading these scriptures.

Colossians

3:1, set your heart on things above not one earthly things. 3. For you did (the old you) and your life is now hidden with

Christ in God. 5. Tells us whatever belongs to our earthly nature must be put to death. 7. Tells us we are not to walk in the way that we once lived. 8. We must rid of anger, rage, malice, slander and filthy language. 9. Tells us not to lie on each other since we have taken off our old self with its practices. 10. Having put on the new self which is being renewed in knowledge in the image of its creator.

Knowing what God has to say about us, and how He sees us should be enough to make us find out for ourselves.

Genesis 1:27 we are created in God's image.
Deuteronomy 28:13 we are the he's and not the tail.
Psalm 17:8 we are the apple of God's eye.
Ephesians 1:7 we have been set free.

This is how God sees us, so we should see our self the same way. A new mind brings with new thinking. We can find comfort in God's Word because, Hebrews 4:12 for the word of God is alive and active sharper than any double-edged sword, it penetrates even to dividing soul and spirit.

When we know better, we do better. It is not enough to receive the truth of God. We must walk in it; we must walk in it! We must live it, breathe it, speak it and it will set us free! It is the sin that keeps us in bondage and only when we have allowed the truth to drive out the sin can we be free.

When you are at the crossroad of life, that is the best time to reach out and with a sincere heart call out to your Heavenly Father for true wisdom- not man, woman or anything else but God. It is God that gives us the wisdom that we need to make the right choices to move on to the next part of our journey walking toward heaven.

JACQUELINE ALLEN

5

PRAISE HIM

Praise Him! Praise God and only Him because He and only He is worthy to be praised. We don't know how good God is until we start sending up the Praises. When the Praises go up the blessings come down. There have been times in my life when I didn't know where my next meal was coming from, the bills were piling up and I didn't know how I was going to pay them. I was sitting around thinking of different excuses that I would tell the bill collector, then it hit me, instead of complaining about what I don't have, start thanking God for who He is and the things that He and only He could do. I remembered how excited I would be when someone would bless me, how I would thank them with all my heart, so I decided to start thanking God daily for waking me up in my right mind for giving me the use of my arms and legs for being my bread, so I would not be hungry a being that never-ending Fountain so I would not be thirsty. I started praising God for who he is and he started blessing me to the point that I had more than enough. I learn how to thank and praise God for all my blessings weather it'd be a smile, a hug, a handshake or a friendly word. When you are truly able to thank and praise God you will feel how special the blessings are to you and you will be able to praise God to the highest and the blessings really will fall Out of Heaven storehouse.

> *Where can you find a better friend than Jesus?*
> *No where!*
> *Where can you find someone who truly love you better than Jesus?*
> *No where!*
> *Who can you find to provide everything you need other than Jesus?*
> *No one!*
> *Who will give up their life for you other than Jesus?*
> *No one!*

Jesus is the answer to all these questions so who deserves praise like Jesus? No one Jesus he's worthy to be praised today tomorrow and forever as long as you have breath in your body you should praise the Lord Psalms 150 and 6 let everything that has breath praise the Lord. There is no one on earth who can do You Like Jesus Does. He loves cares provides comfort and forgives. He's our light protector guidance and a way maker. So, there is no one on earth that deserves the Praises Like Jesus does. The best Praise You can give is to praise God for who He is He's our Rock our Shield our Light our Protector.

Matthew 6:33 tells us to seek his kingdom and everything else will be added for you. Praising and depending on God for everything is the key to the victory we need every single day of our life. Don't let anything or anyone get in the way of your praying and praising God. Don't let anyone stop you from growing because no one would ever do or care for you like God. Surround yourself with people who will pray and praise God with you.

6

WE ARE VICTORIOUS

Things are going to come up on us that we have no control over. God never said that
the weapon would not form but he we can find our comfort and knowing that it will not harm us Isaiah 54:17 no weapon formed against us will prosper and we will refute every tongue that accuses us. John 14:27 say Jesus tells us that all of our troubles are passing and nature for a season and a reason. He tells us not to let our hearts be troubled. We are to hold on to the piece that God gives us being confident that he is watching directing and caring for us because we trust and believe in him.

To be victorious we have to train our minds to block out things that do not concern us. The only thing I want to hear is how God got a person over and through whatever it is that they have faced in their life. God is saying to us Isaiah 26:3, we will keep in perfect peace all who trust in him. That gives us victory! Because it is a comfort knowing that the peace that God gives to us is not like the Peace of the world. The Peace of the world is defined by feelings. But Godly peace is faith knowing that no matter what, God will take care of us. God provided us a whole suit to put on to protect us.

Ephesians 6:10-20 as we are strong, we are to be strong in him and his mighty power.

11. we have to put on the whole armor of God

12. We have to realize our struggle.

14. We have the belt of truth and the breastplate of righteousness.

15. We got to stay ready to run for peace

16. We have our Shield of faith.

17. The helmet of salvation and a sword is what God has equipped us with to have a Victorious Life.

We have to sleep victory! Walk in victory and have faith as small as a mustard seed. Matthew 17:20 Faith as small as a mustard seed can move mountains. We can't change what will happen or what we'll face in life, but we can give it to God. Lay it down at his feet and leave it there. My prayer for us, is that we find peace and victory in our life. We will only make a mess of things when we try to fix things on our own. But when we give it to God, we can walk away shouting victory is mine! Knowing who God, is and how much he loves us we can face anything, because of the power of the cross.

In order to have real victory we have to lay down our life pick up our cross and follow Jesus. James 4:7 tells us to submit ourselves to God and resist the devil and he will flee from us. John 14:27 tell us Jesus gave us his peace and that will give us a Victorious Life. In our life we can't be afraid. 2 Timothy 1:7 God did not give us a spirit of fear but a spirit of power of love and of self-discipline. We have to get serious about our work and what we are called to do for God. In order for us to share our Victory with others we must claim it for ourselves. No matter what you go through or face in this life remember God is with you and that will give you victory. In this life there are so many things that will get in our way to keep us from reaching the Finish Line. Don't stop in this race. Keep going. Life has a way of making things look good and we feel like this is what we have been waiting on so we slack up on the prayers the praise and the pushing for our higher calling but I am saying to you don't give up don't back off just take one more step toward your victory. The finish line is Jesus and I am a living witness if I had stopped when life was pressing down on me, I would not know the wonderful feeling that I have known. Being in a relationship with Jesus is the best choice I ever made in my life.

Jesus Over All!

Jesus my all and all. I can't wait to cross over and stand in front of Jesus to hear him say those famous words, "My child because you endured, welcome my good and faithful servant!"

All that I am and all that I have belongs to Jesus because my victory was with him. Once you surrender your life to God you will be able to withstand the flaming arrows that come your way. Surrendering your life to God will be one of the best decisions that you could ever make in your life. You will fall on your knees and jump up shouting victory is mine!

7

FOOD FOR THOUGHT

FEED YOUR HEART!
Jesus is the bread of life John 6:35
Jesus will provide Matthew 6:25-34
Jesus Loves You John 3:16
You are blessed Matthew 5:3- 12
You are never alone Hebrews 13:5
Victory is yours Roman 8:37
Don't worry Philippians 4:6
Jesus is our Fortress Proverbs 18:10
Fix your eyes on Jesus Hebrews 12:2
Jesus is our helper Psalms 54 4
God has a plan Jeremiah 29:11
Jesus is a rock Psalms 18 2
Jesus Is a Good Shepherd John 10:11
God will supply all your needs Philippians 4:19
God is for you Ezekiel 36 9
Jesus is our strength Psalms 27:14 and Philippians 4:13
God will perform for you Psalm 57 and Philippians 1:6

It pays to wait things out before you make a rushed decision. Be aware that there are consequences to our actions. We know right from wrong. If we do right then right will follow. If we do wrong then know there is a consequence we got to face because of our actions.

Stop in the Name of Love!
Twelve Stops that Will Contribute to a Greater You

1. Stop complaining about what you don't have start thanking God for what you have watch how much more you gain
2. Stop complaining about the work you have to put in to whom much is given much is required. There's someone out there praying for you opportunity.
3. Stop complaining about haters. There is no such thing as success without critics. No one strives for Perfection will come without persecution.
4. Stop complaining about the attention you invite. If you advertise yourself a certain way people are going to inquire about what's being advertised. Does it matter if they are other things in the store, they came for what they saw on the ad.
5. Stop looking for reasons to talk down on others. You're only making yourself look worse than the people you talk about. Hurt people hurt people.
6. Stop being jealous and envious of other people's progress. Sometimes you might just be more well-off than the person you're envious up. Other times they are only more

well-off because they are busy working while you're busy envious. Get to work!
7. Stop competing. Life is not one big competition. It's not about who has the nicest this or that. It's not about who has the most money. Life is about elevation which leads to Salvation. As God elevates you allow him to use you to elevate others. As he saves you. Allow him to use you to save others. That's life that's love!
8. Stop making excuses for always choosing low-quality mate. If you are constantly attracted to the wrong types and attracting the wrong type it is a lust issue. You have a lust issue that keeps you attracted to the wrong things or people and lust attracts lust. So that's why people are attracted to you it's not rocket science it's the truth.

9 stop dating aimlessly. If a goal is not marriage from the start there should be no start. What exactly are you investing in yourself?

10 stop acting married with folk you aren't married to and let God approve your spouse before you make them your spouse heartbreak and broken home prevention.
11 stop holding grudges you seeing every day and God forgives you every day. Yet, you hold things over people head.
12 stop trying to please everybody and not please God. Please God and let him deal with everybody else. God deserves that much does he not?
-Darryl Stanfield

In all that we do we should acknowledge God and not lean or depend on our own understanding. Dear Lord be a God to us and lead us to the person place and thing you would have us to deal with. Put O Lord the words in our mouths and teach us to speak them. Help us O Lord so that everything in our lives would line up with your will. Amen there are some people that enter into our life that you will never forget and then there are some that you will never remember some good some bad some for a reason that we don't know but God does. Feed your heart with positive thoughts and let God take care of the rest.

8

STAND FIRM!

Math of Life

Add Jesus to your life Romans 10:9-10 multiply your good deeds 2 Corinthians 10:8 divide your blessings with others 2 Corinthians 9:11 subtract all your fears 1Peter 5:7 and that equals to A Wonderful Life Psalm 16:11 the struggles were real getting to where I am now.

There has been sickness, death and all kinds of pain and that caused me to cry out the Jesus and I have been crying out to him ever since and he have never failed me yet. So, I say stand firm in your face for Jesus! I would rather live my life with Jesus as head, then to have all the friends in the world. I heard my pastor say I am a Jesus junkie; I am hooked on him. I feel the same way and I need more and more of Jesus to keep me up. I can't get enough! I would rather have Jesus more than all the silver and gold. When Jesus is the head of your life you can rest assured that he has the last and final say. So, over all things so stand firm in your faith. See it is through my pain that I got to know Jesus in a real and personal way and it is because of my fresh start that I chose to stay with him until I die. Because of Jesus I can truly be myself and be true to him and myself.

No more masks Jeremiah 17:7-8 blessed is the one who trusts in the Lord, whose confidence is in him. I am standing firm because God has a plan, God has a dream, God knows my destiny. I am standing firm because the old me, the send for me is gone. I have been renewed, mind, soul and body. I could have should have would have been dead and gone dying in my sin had it not been for Jesus. He saw something in me that I couldn't see. He stayed right by my side and never left me. God has a plan and a purpose for each of us. I am still a work in progress but Jesus stood with me and now I am standing firm in him. I shall not be moved. The joy of victory in times of challenge remind us that God is truly sufficient for whatever life may throw at us.

Romans 8:28 and we know that all things work together for good to them that love God, to them who are called according to purpose. Stand firm on God's promise because it is his goodness and care that can teach us that overcoming is possible because Psalm 136:1 tell us God's love endures forever. In order to believe that God is working all things for our good, then one of the great challenges is to allow hard painful and tearful experiences to be our teacher, in the classroom of life.

James 1:2-4 consider it pure joy my brothers whenever you face trials of many kinds because you know that the testing of your faith develops perseverance. Perseverance must finish its work so that you may be mature and complete not lacking anything. Everything happens in our lives for a reason and a great part of that reason is to help us grow in our space. As to give us the strength to stand firm.

We have to trust in the loving purpose of a sovereign God. We must trust that he is in control when life seems to be out of control.

2 Corinthians 5:7 for we walk by faith, not by sight. In order for us to stand firm we have to believe that God is able to handle the things that are going on in our lives. Sometimes we try to figure out what others want from us and it can be very frustrating. All God wants from us is to do justly, love mercifully and to walk humbly with him. God desires us to do the right thing. We are to love others as he has loved us, but we are to follow him. He asked that we walk with a humble spirit. God does not want us to be afraid to come to him even when we make mistakes. He wants us to come to him so he can help us overcome any sins that we may be struggling with and I allowed him to guide our lives. That is what God's love is. It is there to remove our fears and build our confidence in him and him alone. There is no one on Earth that we can stand firm before that will love us unconditionally, forgive us fully, take care of all our needs no one to do that but God. So, stand firm before God.

9

GOD NAMED US

While we were still in our mother's womb. Already knew the name he had picked out for us. God is the reason why even in our pain we can smile. He loves us unconditionally and his mercy and Grace is renewed every day. Name changes on you, but God never will he stays the same always. God look beyond our faults and saw our needs. He reached way down and pulled us up out of the Miry clay and for that I am very grateful. God named us and it is time for us to start living up to our name. When God sent his only son to take our place on the cross and he rose again on the third day for all those that believe and accept him we became new. When Jesus did what he did for us our name change. I believe that my new name came when I lay down my life and picked up my cross to follow after Jesus. It was after Jesus Took the weight off my cross that I was able to carry it. Picking up my cross put a desire in my heart to wants to know who God was and who I was to him.

GOD IS..

STARTING OVER

Jehovah- Elohim the Eternal creator
Jehovah-Jireh the Lord will see and provide.
Jehovah-Rapha, the Lord our healer.
Jehovah -Shalom, the Lord our peace.
Jehovah -Tsidkenu, the Lord our righteousness.
Jehovah- Mekoddishkem, the Lord our sanctifier.
Jehovah- Shammah, the Lord is present.
Jehovah –Elowyn, the Lord most high
Jehovah-Rohi, the Lord is my shepherd
Jehovah- Hoseenu, the Lord our maker
Jehovah-Eloheenu, the Lord our God

Now that we know some of his names, it is time for us to learn our name. God let us know we are loved. He knows us so much that every hair on our head it's counted. We are the apple of his eyes. He is King So that makes us prince and princess, we are a new creation, we are chosen, we are redeemed, we are hopeful, we are anointed, we are forgiven we are unique of all of God's creation, nothing can replace you. After taking on our new names we can find true love, true peace and true comfort knowing who we are to God. Any Other Name that we are called if they don't line up with the names that God has given you then you don't even have to answer to them, but we do have a God-given duty to live up to our God given name. Knowing who we are in God will cause us to stand. Don't fold under criticism rise up to it and use it as a few or to accomplish your God-given dream. In following out your dream there will be testing but without the test you will never grow. You can make failure be your service because God can use it for his good. I know that you know your name God only wants you to give him your best. Isaiah 43:18-19 God is saying to us to forget the former things, do not dwell on the past. See I am doing a new thing

2Corinthians 5:17 God is saying to us since you are in Christ you are a new creation the old has gone, the new has come. New Life in Christ, new house which is your body. 2 Corinthians 4:8 -9 God is saying to us we may be hard pressed on every side but not crushed, perplexed but not in despair, persecuted but not abandoned, struck down but not destroyed 2 Corinthians 4:16-18 God is telling us to keep our eyes fixed on Things Not Seen because what is unseen is eternal Isaiah 40:31 God is telling us to keep our hope in him and he will renew our strength we will be able to and not be weary. Isaiah 41:10 God is saying to us we do not have to fear because he is with us always Isaiah 54-17 God is saying to us to walk with him and no weapon Force against us shall Prevail. Knowing our God-given name and living up to them God is saying to us and 2Corinthians 5:9 to make it our goal to please him no matter what and everything will be well in our life. It is time to lose the baggage that has been holding us back we all have things in our lives that we hold on to, things that slow us down, things that prevent us from moving forward. If we never let them go, then we will have too much to carry. Now that we know who God is we can lay it all down at his feet and leave it there. God love us and he desires to have a relationship with us. Don't let anything stand in your way from having that relationship with him.

10

GOD OPENED MY EYES

For the biggest of my life, I was walking around with my eyes closed. Not my fleshly eyes but my spiritual eyes. I could not move forward in life because I was looking at all the things that was happening to me and all the things that was happening around me. Once I took my eyes off all the Earthly things, I was able to see all the things that God was really trying to show me. Once I open my spiritual eyes my health started to get better, I was able to come off all that medicine that I was on that always made me feel worse anyway. Once I opened my eyes and started looking at God everything started looking different. Now, I can do all things through Christ who strengthen me Philippians 4:13. Where I once said I can't handle this or that, I began to say, "I am more than a conqueror!" I have figured it out, that, while I was sitting around worrying about it, God, had already worked it out! Through my natural eyes, I was too blind to see it. But now, through my spiritual eyes, I can see it and praise God for blessing me beyond anything I could ever think or imagine. Before I started to see I could not stand on faith because I was using fear as a crutch. Once I began to see I realize that the Pains of life was only for to strengthen me. I realize that the trials were only a test that would later become my testimony. Amazing Grace I once was blind but now I see. I was once lost but now I'm found. Amazing Grace how sweet the sound that saved a Wretch like Me. A lot of times we see things the way we want to see them but in order for us to have a real life we got to get focused and start seeing things that God want us to see. If you can't see God, you cannot please him. The ways of seeing things clearly are by Renewing Your Mind once we do that we can see better, talk better, walk better and act better because seeing the things of God help us to want to do better. Don't base your situation or circumstances on how you see someone handling there's because it will cause you to lose sight every time. Whatever is for them it's for them and whatever is for you is for you. God has a blessing with our name on it continue to look and keep your eyes focused on God so you would not let your blessing pass you by. Now I am seeing walking talk and testimony. Says My Eyes Are Open I no longer push the people away that God sent to help me. Now that I can see everyone is not the same, that hurts even feels different.

Where I once sat around and cried now, I can raise my voice and praise God for he is so worthy of all Praises. Glory Glory Hallelujah Hallelujah since I laid my burdens down. I feel better so much better! I want the world to know that I was one of the blind women that God gave sight to. Peace is what I was thinking and I am sure that one point in your life you are seeking it also. Jesus gives that unexplainable peace that we are seeking, it is that piece that will guard our hearts in mind. No more will we have an anxious heart. We are promised that the peace of God and we can rest easy. Philippians 4:6 be careful for nothing but in everything by prayer and supplication with Thanksgiving let your requests be made known unto God.

STARTING OVER

11

GOD WILL CARRY US THROUGH

Today I speak the word of God over our life in our circumstances. We will not be destroyed we will not be defeated we would not be bound The Lord Is Our Shepherd we shall not want he lays down in Green Pastures and lead us by the Sea of waters. He restores our soul no harm will come near us or our family. No weapon formed against us can prosper because we are covered and kept under the blood of Jesus. When we choose to remain in the presence of God, we make him feel at home in our hearts. I know God will carry us through because his battle does not belong to us 2nd Chronicles 20:15 the Lord say to us do not be afraid or discouraged because of this vast Army for the battle is not yours but God. So, give it to God and let him handle it. God can turn things around for us. Don't lose hope, out of every disaster God can bring a new beginning. Who do you know in your life that can turn midnight in today other than God? Who do you know in life that even the wind and the waves obey them other than God. Believe in God and watch him show his glory in your life John 11:40 Jesus said did I not tell you that if you believe you will see the glory of God.

STARTING OVER

God can and he will bring us through whatever comes against us in life. Romans 8:37 tells us that we are more than conquerors. God has a plan for us Jeremiah 29 11 through 13 tells us about God's plan and the thoughts he has toward us. 11 for I know the thoughts that I think toward you said the Lord thoughts of peace and not of evil to give you an expected in 12 then show you call upon me and you shall go and pray unto me and I will hear you. 13 and you shall seek me and find me when you search for me with all your heart. In order for God to bring us through we have to keep our minds and hearts focus on him. We got to be still and know that he is God. You can be still because God is active, you can rest because God is busy Psalms 37:7 says wait patiently on the Lord. Delight yourself in God and he will bring rest of your soul Psalm 46 10 Psalm 37:7 Isaiah 40:31 God has equipped us to handle life as it comes which is why he tells us to only focus one day at a time. Set your mind on God and what he has placed in front of you and let him take care of the rest. Isaiah 26:3 God is saying to us we will keep in perfect peace all who trust in him there is hope and comfort in knowing that the peace that God gives you no one can take it from you. There is hope in knowing who God is and that he loved you very much. There is hope and knowing that we can face anything life throws at us because of the power of the Cross. We have the cleanest iHeart of all the hate that would cause drama, anything in our life that would disrupt our peace we have to let it go. God dwells in us as a result of his love. We have accepted the spirit of God to reside in us so that means that we are subjected to his counsel and his guidance. What does this mean it means we are not slaves to our selfish desires or craving. We are now able to rise above them and leave according to the way of the spirit then we can find that true peace that we are searching for. We have to always seek God will for our lives and not the selfish demands that we want wanted. Two elements of our growth are Mercy and Truth these are the elements of our moral character and what we should strive for as believers. They should be with us throughout our lives, we should write them on our heart and keep them close at hand. They are also a part of that true peace that we are searching for. God is Mercy and truth so we practice it, we are like him when we practice it, we will be pleasing to God and we will also be prized by man instead of getting angry at someone pray for them don't let anything called you your peace. When you pray for someone who has mistreated you and you are genuine about it, you take back the power of your peace and God knows your heart. It could cause them to set free to your prayers so they can find true peace in their lives. Prayers change thing prayers bring peace.

12

FALL BACK AND SPRING FORWARD

Every year for the past five years, during the fall, I go down. And when the spring comes, I'll be out and about trying to do things I believe God has shown and spoken to me to carry out. I am up trying to tell someone or show someone that he's able to do more than we can ask or imagine. There has been many of roadblocks put in my way. The fight has been real and there were times that I saw no way out, only to realize that this matter was not mine. All I had to do was obey and believe. The voice in my head said open the door. OH, I was fighting so hard not to fall, I fell hard. I hit the floor and realize that it was Fall time. This has gone on for years, but this year was different. I got knocked down with a renewed understanding.

Do you believe that there is a need, a must that we have to renew our understanding almost daily? Sometimes our thinking gets ahead of us and we have to take out time to renew our minds. Renewing our minds mean renewing our understanding. There is not one thing that was done in our life that we can go back and change. So, we always got to keep our eyes focused on the prize that God has for us. The past is gone, tomorrow may never come so focus on today and the things that you can do now but always keep in mind that the only things that are going to last are the things of God. Everything else will fade away.

It is time for a fresh new start in life. So, we have to Ephesians 4:22-24 put off our old self which belongs to our former manner of life and is corrupt through deceitful desires and put on our new self-created after the likeness of God and true righteousness and Holiness. It is important for us as Believers to understand that all of our actions begin with a thought. We must take hold of our thoughts. In order to start life over we must consider Philippians 4:8 finally Brethren whatsoever things are true whatsoever things are honest whatsoever things are pure whatsoever things are lovely whatsoever things are of good report if there be any virtue and if there be any praise think on these things.

God is the answer to everything we need or want. He holds the Whole World in His Hands. Sometimes when you feel the weight of the world on your shoulder and you feel so overwhelmed that you don't know what to do I encourage you to fall back and spring forward with God leading you. I know that when all else fails you can truly trust God. He's a mind regulator. He's a heart fixer. He's Alpha and Omega. No matter what you are going through God will deliver you. He said he would never leave you nor forsake you. He's a rock and He is our Shield. He's our strength when we are weak. Jesus is a way maker, burden Bearer and a heavy load Sharer.

Bounce up knowing that you can trust Jesus He's our God and our strength. He keeps us when the world and the things of the world rise up against us. We have to humble ourselves under the mighty hand of God, he cares for us. God wants us to come to him he's able to handle any struggles that we are dealing with. Trust God and allow him to guide your life. God promise to hold us in his hand. He keeps us in his loving arms and he answers us that everything is going to be alright. Always pray for others, because someone pray for us. Great is the Lord and He is greatly to be praised and his greatness is unsearchable. When we are walking in God's path, God will always confirm his word to the people in our lives who need to know.

Thank God and Thank You!

To My Church Family GRACE BAPTIST,
I am forever grateful for you all! A Special thanks to my Pastor, Jermal Boddie, Sr., Minister Amy Deanes, Deacon Arthur Walker and all other members that are always supporting me.

My Prayer Warriors: Lori Dreux; my sister, James Pierce; my brother, Issac Bean; my son, Shirley Pierce; my aunt, Amy Deanes; my sister and Charlotte McHenry; my Godmother.

I want to give a special shout out to my MOTIVATORS!!! My Cousins: Dianne, Evonne, Elaine, and Joyce Rogers and my son Cedric Pierce.

Bible- King James Version

Stanfield, Darryl (year unknown) Stop in the Name of Love! Twelve Stops that Will Contribute to a Greater You